12 Principles Of Personal Growth

Bringing Meaningful Change To Your Life

Anisa Marku

Copyright © 2019 by Anisa Marku
12 Principles of Personal Growth

All rights reserved. No part of this publication may be reproduced, distributed or transmitted in any form or by any means, including photocopying, recording, or other electronic or mechanical methods, without the prior written permission of the author, except in the case of brief quotations embodied in critical reviews and specific other noncommercial uses permitted by copyright law.

Although the author has made every effort to ensure that the information in this book was correct at press time, the author does not assume and hereby disclaim any liability to any party for any loss, damage, or disruption caused by errors or omissions, whether such errors or omissions result from negligence, accident, or any other cause.

Adherence to all applicable laws and regulations, including international, federal, state and local governing professional licensing, business practices, advertising, and all other aspects of doing business in the US, Canada or any other jurisdiction is the sole responsibility of the reader and consumer.

The author does not assume any responsibility or liability whatsoever on behalf of the consumer or reader of this material. Any perceived slight of any individual or organization is purely unintentional.

The resources in this book are provided for informational purposes only and should not be used to replace the specialized training and professional judgment of a health care or mental health care professional.

The author cannot be held responsible for the use of the information provided within this book. Please always consult a trained professional before making any decision regarding treatment of yourself or others.

Dedication

This book is dedicated to:

My favorite people in the world, my family! Thank you for inspiring and supporting me.

&

To everyone that is still in the "work-in-progress" phase. Keep loving, laughing, and learning.

"Continued improvement is better than delayed perfection."

- Mark Twain

Contents

Introduction 1

Chapter 1: Failure Is Your Best Teacher 3

Chapter 2: Follow Your Path - Don't Chase the Crowds 9

Chapter 3: Find Your Voice - In Life - At Work - At Home 15

Chapter 4: Set SMART Goals 19

Chapter 5: Plan Ahead, But Leave Room For The Unexpected 29

Chapter 6: The 3 C's: Confidence, Commitment, Courage 33

Chapter 7: Be a Good Listener - Talk Less, Listen More 37

Chapter 8: Make Yourself a Top Priority - Self Care 41

Chapter 9: Let Go of Things That Hold You Down: 45

Chapter 10: Embrace Challenge 53

Chapter 11: Do a SWOT Analysis on Yourself 55

Chapter 12: Stop Judging Yourself and Start Observing 59

Bonus 61

Acknowledgments 63

About The Author 64

Introduction

When pursuing any venture in life, starting out may seem confusing, overwhelming, and unattainable. Through the experiences and guidance of this book, you can find clarity and confidence by setting organized, reachable, and beneficial goals for yourself by creating healthy mental habits.

By accepting past failures, turning self-doubt and external influences into determination and learning organizational techniques to make time for your purpose, we can see a more precise, brighter horizon on our path to success.

Throughout each step to personal development, you will be provided one core concept in each chapter so you can build each skill upon the next.

You will find common ground with the stories and insights throughout each chapter to provide the support you need to continue your journey of personal growth.

Chapter 1
Failure Is Your Best Teacher

> *"Failure is success in progress."*
> -Albert Einstein

The best teaching lessons in life come from past failures. Sometimes people react to their failures as "the end." Instead, it should be seen as a step closer to success. We start something - we make mistakes - then we quit because it didn't work out as we wanted to. We think we have failed, which is why most don't even bother to try again. They result in quitting without going back to the drawing board to make their dreams reality. We all share this common ground of failure. This is when we are presented with two forks in the road: giving up or retrying. It is only with our perseverance do we define ourselves as the victims of our failures or becoming resilient. The resilient mind considers that if our mistakes beat us down, the least we can say is we learned from it.

Are you starting a new relationship, career, or business venture? Will you give up and stop as soon as something goes wrong? Or will you keep going and take all the lessons from previous experiences to improve and succeed in your next move? These choices are what determine the outcomes of our goals. These are examples of the options life presents us that reveal the essence of our character, drive, and desire towards our objective.

Whatever your failures may be, whether they involve friendships, relationships, or career choices; when you quit, then you have failed.

Everything we go through teaches us a lesson. Each lesson of life should provide us with a mindset. As humans, we should always be changing and evolving to a more advanced, progressed, and disciplined sense of self-being, but this is not always the case. Sometimes life is trying to teach us something, but when we fail, we look at it as "the end." The belief that the first failure determines our outcome can become our crutch. We depend on this being the only option because our defeats do not make us feel comfortable. When we come to terms with the fact that our failures are unpleasant, it provides us with the motivation to relieve that by reattempting, which ultimately leads to success.

The wrong mentality that is instilled in us throws us into a negative feedback loop of submission to our insecurities and self-doubt that only keep us going backward. The origin of our hesitations is from how we perceive and connect to our misfortunes.

Think about a time in your life that you have thought you failed at your overall goal.

Write it down.

What did you learn from it?

Write down at least three things that you learned from that experience.

What are they? How can you take those lessons and implement them in your life right now?

We hang on to negative thoughts and negative experiences that do not allow us to move forward. If we keep it that way, we either take steps backward or we standstill. Either way, we are not moving forward, which means no growth. That is not where we belong - where our process of evolution is at a standstill, and our desire to grow is flooded with self-doubt.

Every day is a new day new - you don't look at the calendar and mark off the same day every day, right? We have to move forward, one step at a time, one day at a time.

Dropping out of high school was the biggest regret in my life for many years. With a self-perception as being inferior to those around me, it caused self-doubt in my sense of feeling like a good person, mother, and wife. I dropped out of high school at sixteen. My previous years of education were either paused or skipped due to moving many times during my childhood. Between the gaps in my education and moving to America at just 18 years old where I had to assimilate into the culture, language as well as becoming a first-time mom, my self-doubt caused great strain on my self-identity and how I thought others perceived me. At that age, I experienced many life milestones quickly while still trying to grasp my self-view of the world around me. Through all this, the voice of my regret influenced my opinion of myself.

The most ashamed I felt would be when people would ask, "Where did you finish school?" I would stare back, pause for a long time and then answer with half of my voice, "I did not."

As the years went by, my desire of getting a full education would still ring in the back of my head. As that ambition grew louder, the more I started to become aware of the opportunities that I had. After some research and drive to find the motivation within myself, suddenly "my education" was not impossible to achieve. There was still hope.

I know for many people there may be some surprise or confusion as to how I did not register sooner with the ease of the accessible education America has in this era, but it's not as simple as one may think.

First, I didn't have anyone in my inner circle to teach me that. Being in a world surrounded by the fact that no one around me had gone past high school made it a challenge to realize the attainability of my education. Second, for eight years, I had to work on getting my permanent residency here in the USA.

When applying for college if you are not a permanent resident, you are considered as an international student in such cases, tuition prices sometimes triple. Also, I didn't want to start college and then suddenly have to leave the country and drop out again.

When you are going through the process in and out of immigration courts, your outcome is unsure, and nothing is certain regarding approval of residency. My husband and I came to the U.S. almost sixteen years ago; it took us eight years to receive our permission for residency and fourteen years to become US citizens. It is a long, stressful, time consuming and expensive process. However, if you follow all the steps, you are required, it is well worth the work.

Third, I had two kids and no one to watch them. I had to wait until they both started school full time to be able to start college. I started college in 2012 at my local community college and graduated two years later with my associates in liberal arts and general business. After that summer, I transferred to Walsh College to get my BA in business. I graduated from Walsh in June of 2017.

I faced many obstacles during these five years. My life was filled with so many predeterminations not to pursue my goal. I had many reasons to desert my aspiration due to the multitude of responsibilities and stressors in which gave me many reasons to throw in the towel.

But I didn't, and I am so grateful that I didn't stop or gave up on myself and that I now have the ambition to inspire others.

Between raising two kids, one miscarriage and having two more babies, the list is not short of challenges that it took to preserve. But I had an intention- a dream important enough for that I concluded that abandoning just wasn't an option. I continued one step a time (small steps), but I kept moving forward, and that helped me with making it all possible.

Failing was not an option. My past failures had taught me what failure feels like, and it provided the drive not to give up on graduating.

I had given up on my education when I decided to drop out of school. However, through the years of longing to attain my education, I turned my self-doubt into the courage I needed to jump off the deep end whether I failed or prevailed. That taught me that no matter what it takes, no matter what you are going through in life- if your goal is important enough, you will find a way to overcome everything that life presents you.

There is no failure in life. You will either succeed, or you learn.

When we fail, there is a feeling of not being good enough or smart enough, and that prevents us from trying again. It hampers our ambitions to give something our full force because we feel like we are undeserving of it, due to the previous failure, which leads us to not giving it our all and missing out on prime opportunities to fly.

If we let the fear of failure take control of our thoughts, then we will end up doing only ordinary things. We will never really go after what we want because the fear of failure controls us. If we look at each failure of our lives as a teaching moment or teaching lessons, we will also get rid of the fear of failure. There is no failure. There are only lessons.

Sometimes we have people around us (even at a young age) that intentionally or unintentionally instill the fear of failure in us. For me, it was my teacher. As a first-grader, I remember there was a lot of abuse in our classroom, school, and it was considered "normal," and in many cases, the parents even encouraged it.

Every day, I remember as a kid being horrified to go to school because even though I studied and did all my homework, I was still scared that I would fail and be "punished." So every single day, I made sure I was prepared for school, yet I entered my classroom with the same anxiety of inferiority and fear of failure.

No child in any part of the world should get up in the morning and go to school horrified from fear that they might fail, ever. Due to the time and place I grew up in, that was the harsh reality of a young student's life. I believe if our teachers and our parents would have taught us a different approach to being a good student as well as put into perspective that failing a test or assignment is not the end of the world certainly my classmates and I would have entered the classroom with a different feeling. If that were the case, we might have been more excited to learn, and with that, we may have had confidence even if we struggle with a lecture or assignment.

Next time you think of yourself as you have failed at something, look at it from a different perspective. Learn from it, grow and keep going.

Chapter 2
Follow Your Path - Don't Chase the Crowds

"The one who follows the crowd will usually get no further than the group. the one who walks alone is likely to find himself places no one has ever been."

- Albert Einstein

We tend to follow the group everywhere we go. The issue is we follow only the crowd that is around us. We compare and contrast our life to our circle of friends, family, and next-door neighbors. Now with social media, we have the entire world to analyze ourselves against.

Look at five people that you hang out with every day or most of your free time.

Who are they?

What are their fears?

What are their strengths?

What is their background?

What do they do for a living?

What is their religion?

What about their social class?

Are they married?

Do they have kids?

The chances are that you and your close circle have a lot in common and are very similar in many ways.

When I came to the US, everyone I met or had an opportunity to talk with, I would always ask the same questions, "How many years have you been living here? What do you do for a living?"

I was amazed that everyone had built a great life, worked very hard and most of them had bought a house for their family. At that time, all I could think of was, 'When am I going to have what they have? When am I going to be able to buy a house for my kids? When am I going to be able to find a job? I was comparing and wanting for myself the same things as the next person had. Nothing more. I didn't know that there was more and I didn't realize that it was even possible to strive further.

As the years went by, I started to realize that I wanted to finish college to complete my education. I didn't want to get just any job. I wanted a career that I would be happy going to every day.

Had I just followed the crowd I was surrounded with, I probably would have never graduated or even started college. My desire to broaden my horizon affected my overall outcome, and without that motive, I would still be influenced by those around me.

At the age of twenty-six, I began my college journey while raising two children. After earning my associate degree in general business and liberal arts in 2014, the downpour of motivation to pursue my educational path was immense. The same year, I transferred colleges, had two more boys and graduated with my BA, in June of 2017. The laborious sacrifices during the five years of studies were challenging and strenuous, but I would eagerly do it all over again. Looking at the outcome of my quest for achievement, my past struggles and my surroundings became only my fuel to blast off.

In the future when you find yourself with the motivation to do something, buy something, or achieve something, first ask yourself, "Do I want it or is it because someone in my circle has it?"

A typical thirty-year-old female has a family or is starting one, maybe has purchased a house, has already finished her education, has a great job, etc. Nothing wrong with this picture, right? We all might know many people in our circle that have all the above. But there is nothing wrong with being a 30-year old that does not have a husband, or kids, or a home mortgage, or even a 9-5 job either.

If you choose of paying a mortgage instead of traveling, that is your choice, but if someone else has chosen another path, it does not mean that they are wrong or they are wasting their life. On the contrary, they may be much happier and are possibly even more fulfilled in life.

The way other people perceive others is not necessarily reality. Reality is what you need to follow your path, wherever that might lead you.

It is your choice to make

Your consequences to pay

And your lessons to learn.

Again, had I followed people around me, I would have never even applied for college. No one in my circle of friends or family, my parents, my husband, or any of the people I met would have given me the ambition to follow my passion. I had no mentor, no support, no advice to take. All I had was my goal to continue my education and choose my career path.

Many people asked why I was going to college instead of just getting a job many times. After all, with my husband being the only provider, I agree if I had started working our lives as a family would have been a little easier. Two paychecks are better than one, after all. The tension between my obligations as a mother and my intention for desired opportunities left me at a crossroads. I could tell that an entry-level job would leave me feeling incomplete. I was aware of my potential, but I could not hear it. My mind was so preoccupied with my doubt and external forces that I could not listen to where I needed to go. During this time, I learned that the ability to listen to your inner needs by muting all the negativity would light up the path you need to follow.

If you need support and you get refused that's okay too. It might take you a little longer, but you will get there. Once you succeed, go even further.

They will doubt, discourage, even make fun of you, but you can't live, and you should not live your life pleasing people. Making them happy, and forgetting about yourself will only cause you to have regrets in your heart and mind.

People are in different stages of their lives. For example, if you and your friend are reading the same book, and you just began the story while your friend is well into the sixth chapter. Can you enjoy/understand or appreciate the story/book if you skip to the sixth chapter to keep up with your friend?

Starting from the beginning and reading for yourself is the only way you can appreciate and learn from the story at hand.

Even if she tries to give a summary of what she has learned so far, the odds are you won't be able to absorb, welcome and acknowledge all of the lessons and experiences if you do not immerse and read the book yourself.

Learning comes from experience. It comes from your story. When your own story begins, you must start on the first chapter of your journey. You should feel no obligation to skip any pages to be where someone else is.

This part of your story should be a process of self-appreciation, self-reflection, and growth. Living your story in someone else's narrative is a disservice to the flourishment that's already been made from your own past experience. It is an underappreciation of your endurance. By living our truths and ignoring others perceptions of us, we pay homage to the fact that we have survived what we thought we could not, got up when we have had enough and stood strong with grace. Finding that voice and searching for the narrative in your own story is the first step to letting go and building up.

Chapter 3
Find Your Voice - In Life - At Work - At Home.

Finding your voice requires courage, strength, and encouragement. Growing up in a hush-hush culture (mainly revolving around female behavior), I was never allowed to speak up or make independent decisions for myself. Even when I tried, I would be shut down immediately by someone older than me. Growing up as an only child only caused more difficulty, since I didn't have anyone to talk to. So, often, I would completely shut down. If I asked, there was no answer. If I spoke, I would be blamed or made fun off. So it was just more comfortable and more convenient not to talk and listen to others and to follow their voices and their paths.

Feelings of isolation, helplessness, and ostracism can be prevalent when going through this or similar experience. It is only human to react to vulnerability with an attempt to self-soothe. Whether we comply with what other people tell us to do, lash out, or shut-in out our lives from the world, we still have the same issue that we haven't confronted. It's easier to not deal with a feeling like this if it is all you have ever known, or maybe you think it is easier to live your life by of someone else's voice instead of your own.

The way we take this experience and use it to amplify our voice can result in a positive outcome for what we want our aspirations to be. Sometimes, we even find it very difficult to find our dreams and goals because we are so used to doing what other people tell us we should.

When you continuously have exterior opinions around you that want to make decisions for you with different intentions, the route to the person you want to be or the life you want to have may become blurry. Continual judgment may cause negative reinforcement when making different decisions than those around you. This only feeds the cycle of stagnant self-growth due to the attitudes of those you surround yourself with. Breaking that cycle is the only way to find your true meaning.

Let's break down this down further by brainstorming an instance in your life where you felt voiceless. We can start by creating a web. You can use the prompts within the bubbles to get yourself started.

What Was The Experience

That Made You Feel Voiceless?

What/ who was the cause of this experience?

How has it affected your life?

How did it make you feel?

What do you want to change about this experience?

Now elaborate further. Why did it make you feel this way? What are things that you need to reassess about the experience that could help change your way of thinking?
What is the origin of the cause of the experience? Where did it come from/ how did it happen? What has the person experienced themselves to make you feel this way? For example, did they have people who did the same?

What are the new things you would like to learn about yourself? What are the new skills you'd like to have? What are bad habits you want to quit that was acquired from this experience?

What are the things it has taught you? What are the things you can from it? What are the things you can leave behind?

Creating a clear structure of the way you're feeling and brainstorming all aspects of how this issue occurred is a great way to start your road to finding your voice. It is also a great way to deal with any problem you may have to have a concise and explained form of this issue as well as help some emotional healing by providing some explanation to the occurrence which can help clear your path to success.

Granting yourself access to your expression is a strength that can allow you to make your mark on the world around you. In finding your voice, your power begins to outnumber your fears. Overcoming will be the motivation you need to heal yourself so you can achieve the success you were meant to have. To find your expression, you can put your life in terms of a flower. A flower doesn't bloom or wither away because someone is looking at it or approves of it. It blooms because that is what it was meant to do. The same goes for a happy future. Your life shouldn't flourish based on the opinion of others. Your success should be defined by the act of your prosperity, being something you were meant to do. The moment you decide to spend your life by doing and not seeking is the only moment you can unlock your full potential.

Sometimes, living through the voices of other people's opinions for so long gives us a sense of comfortability. We become so voiceless; we forget we have one ourselves. Putting that voice to use after living with the intentions that aren't yours can cause great difficulty in every aspect of your life. Finding that confidence inside yourself will take time. Ironically, it is a journey you take on your own. Choosing your own time and space to do so is an essential factor in creating your individuality. It may be hard, but it will be worth it.

12 Principles Of Personal Growth

Gaining your confidence to break the oppressive barriers from your surroundings takes unfathomable courage. We can achieve this strength through small steps. It ultimately comes down to you to conjure up the bravery to discover your voice. A small way may include speaking for yourself, even when you do not feel confident. Situations like this can provide you with a reminder of the power you've always had within yourself- the power you were unable to hear because others spoke over it and for it. Once you listen to that voice and use its ability to make the decisions you want for yourself and not others creates limitless possibility.

Chapter 4
Set SMART Goals

Setting goals for yourself is the first step you can take to achieve something significant. But don't just write any goals- write SMART goals.

Smart goals are:

S- Specific

M-Measurable

A-Attainable

R-Relevant

T-Timely

Have you ever thought of how your life would change if you accomplished something significant in your life?

Maybe you have been thinking of doing one of the following:

- Changing careers
- Getting your degree
- Gaining financial stability
- Traveling more
- Having a healthier lifestyle

Your goal depends on what you want to accomplish. Think of a few things that are important to you and how it would change your life if you achieved it.

To help you get started, ask yourself :

- What would you change, or how would you make your life better?
- What would make you feel better about yourself?
- What kind of experiences would you like to try in your lifetime?
- Who do you want to become?
- What would you like to have?

Step 1 - Write it all down

I start by putting my thoughts into a notebook. If I don't write them down chances are I will forget them the next day (or next minute).

Whatever comes to mind, quickly write it down. It doesn't have to be a specific goal yet. As long as there's substance, there is something to work toward.

Visualizing the big picture may be difficult at first. A non-intimidating approach to seeing your broad view is to find the end goal and work backward by dividing your big plan into smaller tasks.

One of my personal goals was to graduate college. My "end goal" was to get my degree. Then, I had to divide my goal into smaller, more realistic tasks. By working on those tasks, every single day, every semester, and every year, my "end goal" was accomplished.

My Big Picture:

- Get my diploma

I divided this goal into smaller task per

- Year
- Semester
- Classes
- Test/Assignments

Now it's your turn. What is your big picture? Your end goal? Do a brain dump and write it all down in a notebook. You can write it down on your phone notes or laptop. It doesn't matter as long as you can go back and read it every day.

"Setting goals is the first step in turning the invisible into the visible."
— Tony Robbins

Remember, when setting goals, you need to make sure they are S.M.A.R.T:

Specific

Make it as accurate and detailed as possible. Write down what exactly you want to accomplish.

Measurable

You need to be able to measure your progress. Otherwise, how are you going to know that you achieved your goal?

Attainable

Your goal must be realistic/achievable. You need to have the resources, skills, and the time to achieve your goal.

Relevant

What makes achieving this goal important to you and your life right now?

What or how will that goal improve your life?

Timely

There should be a time frame to accomplish your goal. You need to be a due date after you write your goals down. Otherwise, you are going to be working forever.

S.M.A.R.T goals are the difference between wishing for what you want and accomplishing what you want. Reverting to your notes will help you confirm if your goals are S.M.A.R.T. If they are not, then ask yourself how you can change them. If some of those goals don't meet the criteria and cannot be changed later, you should take them off your list until you can find a way to make them S.M.A.R.T.

Step 2- Divide Your end goal into smaller tasks

Looking at the big picture may be overwhelming and possibly discouraging. Your thoughts may include, "How am I able to achieve that? That is impossible!" But if you divide it into smaller goals or tasks, it doesn't seem so overwhelming.

Going back to my example of getting my degree, I had dropped out of high school at sixteen years old, and I began my college journey at twenty-six with two children. If I had just focused on my end goal, without any real plan, I would have come up with a hundred excuses of how my goal is impossible to achieve, and I would have given up before even starting.

Instead, I divided my goal into more practical tasks, and I focused on those.

I like to divide my goals into categories:
- Personal goals
- Professional goals
- Financial goals
- Business goals
- Travel goals

Fun fact: My travel goal list is longer than the other ones ;)

Some other groups that might be relevant to your goals may be:
- Health & fitness
- Personal growth & development
- Spiritual
- Family
- Social life
- Relationships

I would highly recommend that you start with one category and one goal and then add more as you go along. After you have decided on your category, write down your goal, and apply the SMART method. You can take it one step further and list your goal as a short-term or a long-term goal.

Step 3- Hold Yourself Accountable

You have to remind yourself that no one, except you, is responsible for your success.

You have to put a STOP to excuses
- "I can't do that," or "I don't have time."
- Blaming others
- Negativity from your thoughts
- Negativity from other people

Another suggestion would be finding yourself an accountability partner. An accountability partner is someone that is on the same path as you with the same goals or who loves supporting you no matter what. When I started writing my book and having someone that holds me accountable, and it's on the same path as me, has been really encouraging and helpful.

Step 4- Reward Yourself

Rewarding yourself for every step you accomplish it boosts your confidence with such thoughts like, " I can do this" or " I'm one step closer to reaching my goal." Also, rewarding yourself motivates you and makes all the work even more fun. When I was in college, every semester break, I used to take my boys for a day trip or a long weekend somewhere they liked. I looked forward to spending some quality time with them because I was always studying or doing my homework, even on weekends.

Step 5- Restart and Repeat- Make it a Habit

This whole process can be repeated, and every time you do, it is going to be more comfortable and more exciting when you achieve something, you are passionate about. When you get overwhelmed working towards your goal, keep in mind, "It always seems impossible until it's done." -Abraham Lincoln

Quick Recap:

- Visualize the big picture of what you want to achieve
- Write it down!
- Find your WHY that will motivate you to work on your goals every day
- Make your goal S.M.A.R.T
  - Specific
  - Measurable
  - Achievable
  - Relevant
  - Timely
- Next - Break it down by:
  - Task
  - Time
- Hold yourself accountable
  - Find an accountability buddy
  - Remind yourself that: You are the only person responsible for yourself, your life, and your success
- Don't forget to reward yourself
  - Recognize every step you get closer to your end goal
- Repeat the process - make it a habit
  - Habits are formed
&

12 Principles Of Personal Growth

○ Habits stay with you forever

Do you struggle with staying motivated? Here is a list of 10 ways that I think will help you stay motivated no matter what you are currently working on and what your goals are.

1. Remember WHY you started- always try to remind yourself why you have started. It will keep you going forward if the reason is important enough to you. What are you working on right now? Are you thinking to start your own business? Finish your degree? Or are you trying to be healthier and lose some weight? No matter what you are trying to accomplish, always remember the reason why you are doing it. It might give you the little push that you need to keep going.

2. Reward yourself for every step of the way- Every little step you go forward, give yourself a small reward.

3. Take it one day at a time- one day at a time and one step at a time. That is how it works. You can't do all at once, so take it slowly, one action at a time, and keep moving forward.

4. Get rid of negative people and thoughts that hinder your progress. Instead, surround yourself with positive people and always try to think positively. Stop comparing your progress to others- I have started a course about blogging a few months ago, and one thing that stood out to me was "don't compare your beginning to someone else's middle."

5. Write your progress down on paper-create a vision board. Some people are more visual than others. Vision boards are useful tools to help you see your goals with much more clarity.

6. Eat healthily and be active. Eating healthy and being active is essential for looking and feeling great. When you feel good, you have the desire and the energy to keep up

with everything that needs to be done. Always keep in mind that we could have all kinds of resources at our fingertips, but if we don't use them than they are useless.

7. Don't be scared to fail. Failing is a step of learning and not of giving up or quitting. No one likes to fail. However, there is no other way to learn if we don't fail.

8. Stop procrastinating. I honestly think that procrastination is the biggest enemy. Instead, make a list of things that need to be done and prioritize them.

9. Furthermore, when setting out to achieve your dreams, face each step with a systematic, thorough process. This will prevent discouragement and help weed out any unobtainable approaches. It will also help strengthen your determination. Providing yourself with a strong foundation for what you wish to achieve is a significant key to success in your future endeavors. Assessing, organizing, and determining your goals is the healthiest way to complete your objectives and face any problems head-on.

Chapter 5
Plan Ahead, But Leave Room For The Unexpected

Life happens. Often we plan, and nothing turns out the way we wanted or expected.

Planning and staying organized is necessary and beneficial to your everyday life. We often think that the more you get done, the better you know where you are going. But sometimes we forget that some things are out of our control and realm of change.

We often beat ourselves up about things we can't change instead of focusing on the things we can. This human response is how we deal with the natural responsibility of decision making versus our feeling of invincibility against natural circumstances. Life happens, and we spend so much time and energy on what could have happened that we forget what is happening now.

A way to diagnose when this issue is prevalent in your own life is to ask yourself a simple question, "Is this problem something I can change or cannot change?" Take a moment to ponder and realize that if this problem is something you can change, then great. There is nothing to worry about because there is a way to overcome and achieve. If there isn't something you can do about it- then there is no reason to lose composure because it is out of your hands and therefore not worth your stress. Misinterpreting the power we have over the elements that affect our lives and creating anxiety over things we can't control usually become the foundation of our doubt. Ultimately, this can turn into a domino effect, causing deterioration of your success.

Instead of over-analyzing uncontrollable predicaments, a healthier alternative is to arrange your options in such a way that any hiccups in the road ahead can be faced head-on with confidence and composure. Yes, this sounds much easier said than done. But in enough time, with enough practice, your confidence in your path will provide you with the determination to push through what life throws at you.

I love surprises- for the most part. However, I am a planner and like to have everything in order. Therefore, surprises throw me off and often give me anxiety no matter how beautiful they are.

No matter what type of personality you have or how well organized you are- life happens- and unexpected events throw us off big time.

Examples of unexpected events:

You meet someone new

Health problems

Death in the family

Unique work/career opportunity

Job promotion

Can you think of a time in your life that something very unexpected happened and disrupted your life?

This doesn't necessarily have to be a negative disturbance. A disturbance can be anything unexpected that happens and does not give us any advance notice. Due to the natural abruptness of life, we need to make room for these abruptions and adjust our plans accordingly.

The way we accommodate these circumstances defines how we act upon the hiccups that life presents us. Finding a way to react depends on your life. The best way is to provide yourself with a plan B. Making sure that this plan is just as strong as your original plan will provide you with ease and confidence during your transition to your new plan with confidence.

Sometimes, the effects of an unexpected bump in the road can contribute a sense of vulnerability and insecurity about your goal because you had to change your plans in the first place. Like tripping or falling during a race, we feel like continuing the race to our goal may not be worth trying when down- like we can't catch up — knowing that a change in our plans does not affect the outcome of our success. Your journey may change, but with enough hard work, your destination will not. Plan with confidence in knowing that with enough effort, your goal can be achieved. The key is to continue your journey with the knowledge that your success is inevitable.

Chapter 6
The 3 C's: Confidence, Commitment, Courage

If you want to succeed at anything, commitment is going to be your best friend and procrastination is going to be your biggest enemy. Hold yourself accountable for everything that you do or don't do. Even if you don't have the skills to do something if you commit to it, you will succeed.

Being busy and being productive are two different things. When I ask someone how are you doing the general answer is, "Good, just working - very busy." Although I was in different stages of my life, my answer was almost always the same, "I'm busy..."

When I had one kid and stayed at home.

When I had two kids and was working.

When I had two kids and was going to college.

When I was going to college, working full time and pregnant.

When I had four kids and was going to college.

When I had four kids and was working full time outside the home.

And when I had four kids and was working from home.

We are all busy. There is no doubt about that. But are we productive? How are we managing our time?

That's where the commitment comes in. You may think you don't have time to do what you want because you are very busy as it is. Just try to commit yourself to do whatever it takes to achieve what is on your list. This will result in you prioritizing your goals, which will help you gain time management skills. You will see that once you have your priorities in check, you will commit yourself, and you will find or make time for what is most important.

I had to spend most of my weekends for five years in a row studying, doing homework, and preparing for tests instead of spending with my family because I was committed to graduating. My goal was important enough to me that I had to sacrifice time with my family.

I took advantage of semester breaks to travel with them or go on road trips to spend some quality time. However, during that time had I not been very committed, I would have probably failed or quit 100 times, which in that case. I learned to hold myself accountable.

Making excuses and telling yourself that life is in the way will only take away even further from reaching your goals. It provides you with a way to justify not being motivated and to put your dreams and goals on hold.

Instead, try these steps to stay on track and stay focused on your goal:

1.) Find an accountability partner. Someone that you can count on, who understands your journey and can push you when you feel stuck or unmotivated.

2.) Commit to your schedule, life, and goals.

3.) But also, be careful not to overcommit and don't commit to things that are not important to keep yourself busy or to avoid doing things that need to be done and are a priority. Sometimes we overfill our plates to avoid more critical situations.

Prioritize your life, commit to your list, and hold yourself accountable.

You can do this with:

1.) Confidence: You believe in yourself and grow your inner confidence.
2.) Commitment: You will do whatever it takes to achieve what you want.
3.) Courage: It must be developed. Dare to do anything your way.

By having confidence in yourself and your value, you have a higher chance of success. Knowing you are capable of achieving anything that you put your mind to provides you the courage to stay committed to your goal. Being aware of your truth gives you more of a reason to remain devoted to your cause.

A prime example of how determination transforms commitment is my story of how I went to college. I had the confidence to believe in myself. Commitment helped me go through college. Courage helped me start.

I didn't have any mentors, nor did I have anyone I could look up for encouragement and support. I had to convince myself to take a step at a time and do it. I knew it was essential to me, and I had many "why's" to keep me motivated.

In the beginning, it took me a long time to even apply for college due to my lack of confidence. Lots of questions kept me from going forward, such as, "What if I fail? What if I don't know how to fill out the form? What if my kids get sick and I have to miss school?" My lack of confidence caused me to question myself even before I started to fill out the registration form. If you don't find the courage in yourself to move forward with whatever you are doing in life, you are just going to be running in a circle like a hamster in a wheel. Your overly exaggerated thoughts consume you, and at the end of the day, they are just holding you back. There is nothing you can gain or benefit from overthinking.

Courage means you don't want to stay in your comfort zone anymore. The comfort zone does not mean that you are in a happy place, and you don't need anything to change. It means that that's the only way you know how to live. Anything else besides that means leaving your comfort zone. That is terrifying for some people.

My best friend found the courage to leave an abusive relationship. That takes a lot of courage and strength.

Finding the courage to leave your job, speak up when you need to do the right thing, get help when you need to or overcome the fears that hold you back are just a few examples for when we need to find the courage within ourselves.

Sometimes we think courage is when we go into a situation completely unafraid. But we fail to realize that recognizing our fear and yet not letting that fear stop us is what real courage is. When we find that courage, we get the confidence we need to focus on our goals. Courage shows us the way of who we are.

"The art of conversation lies in listening."

- Malcolm Forbes

Chapter 7
Be a Good Listener - Talk Less, Listen More

"Most people do not listen with the intent to understand; they listen with the intent to reply."
- Stephen Covey

We listen with the intent to reply and give our opinion when we start a conversation. I think our responses would be very different if we stopped thinking about what we are going to respond with and instead truly listen to the other person.

Sometimes, we assume where the conversation is going and immediately cut off the conversation and reply, even though we may not fully understand what the other person was trying to say. Cutting people off shows a lack of respect for the other side of the conversation's feelings and opinions. Plus, if we fail to let the full point of view and notion naturally flow through the conversation, the premature reaction could even cause an argument because the other person meant something else and you interpreted it differently.

If we take the time to listen, sometimes a reply is not as necessary as we think and may not even be asked for. People want to be heard. They want to be able to express themselves without having an answer from another point of view. When their feelings get counteracted with another person's opinion, it makes the person feel invalid comparison to the other side of the conversation.

How does being a good listener helps you as a person?

It helps you in many ways. If you are a good listener, that means that you care and you empathize.

When we have a higher self-awareness of our own words and actions, we realize how they affect others. Self-awareness provides us with stable confidence in our own feelings, which can help validate the feelings of others. Therefore, this balanced self-esteem helps us become the type of listener that we want in other people during our times of self-expression.

Being a good listener helps you build positive relationships in life, career, relationships, and friendships.

You can become a better listener by:

-Practicing mental stillness

-Making remarks or opinions only when positive or necessary

-Thinking before responding

-Remembering that listening is a win/win

-Being attentive and respectful to others ideas, opinions and emotions

-Being present

-Showing empathy

-Practicing open-mindedness

You will have a higher emotional intelligence when practicing these healthy habits. Our emotional intelligence is the awareness of our emotions and the emotions of those around us. If we put it into perspective that these are small practices that we should already be integrating into our common daily courtesies, it makes it easier to achieve becoming a better listener without having to feel we're striving for it.

We have to be okay with not being comfortable. There may be times in your life where you will hear stories or opinions that you might not agree with, or won't like hearing them. Unfortunately, not every single person we talk to has a great happy story to tell us.

When my friend first told me about the abusive relationship she was living in, at first, I honestly didn't want to know. I was not comfortable listening to her due to the thought of how difficult her situation was. At some point during that conversation, I had to stop listening to her. At some times during the conversations, I wished she didn't tell me her story due to the helplessness I felt.

After all, what was I able to do? How was I able to help her?

It is easier for us not to deal with difficult issues. But we need to get out of our comfort zone. If we want people to listen to our hard, painful stories, then we need to listen to others.

Thinking back now, I wish I had been more empathetic and understanding towards her. After she told me the first time, I didn't want to bring back the conversation because it was too uncomfortable for me.

We can't close our ears and eyes when conversations get too uncomfortable. As a friend and as a woman, one thing I could do is listen even if I don't have any advice to give back or any way to help. A lot of times, our mere presence can be the support someone needs during their time of struggle.

In many cases, we don't have any power to change people's situations, but we do have the ability to listen and be understanding. That is sometimes the greatest help of all.

Try to listen because:

-People want/need to be heard.

- By being an active listener, you will learn more about the other person and understand what they are trying to communicate.

- You develop patience, which is very difficult to learn but a precious virtue to have.

- It shows the real strength and self-control you possess.

- You become more compassionate and understandable.

- It improves relationships and earns trust.

- It benefits problem-solving.

- It provides mutual trust in conversations.

- It provides respect and confidence for both sides of the discussion.

When listening, avoid doing the following:

- Jumping to conclusions,

- Missing the point

- Creating unnecessary hostile environments

- Lashing out when in disagreement

- Providing your opinions or stories that revolve around you when people open up to you.

Becoming the listener we want in other people listening to us assists us in setting aside our ego and choosing a selfless input into the lives of other people. To achieve this, we must set simple principles for ourselves in the way we act daily. Becoming a better listener provides us an unbiased goal set to chase our success further.

Chapter 8
Make Yourself a Top Priority - Self Care

To take care of others, you need to take care of yourself first. Self-care is often viewed as selfishness, but it is far from it. When you take care of your health (mentally and physically), you give yourself more energy, desire, and strength to take responsibility, assist, and be there for others.

Self-care is essential for your overall health and boosts your self-esteem. You feel more energetic and productive to make important decisions.

How should we practice self-care?

First, learn how to rest (your body & your mind) instead of just quitting. Burnout happens a lot. I have dealt with it many times throughout my life. It happens when we don't know how or when to pause. However, when we don't get the rest we need mentally or physically, we lack the motivation we need to succeed.

Our bodies and our minds get to the point where they can not take it anymore. We are beyond exhausted from our jobs, our spouses, our children, our to-do list. We feel burned out, and we cannot continue any longer. Then when we quit. We give up.

What happens to the fuse when it is overloading? It just shuts down.

The same goes for people, which results in giving up on the things we tried so hard to obtain.

We must take the time to address where the stress is coming from and take time to re-energize. Learning how to take care of your mental and physical health is a fundamental factor in having a successful path. A healthy mind produces a successful mind, which equals success in your life.

Ever heard the saying "You can't pour out of empty vessels"? It's the same concept. When we are drained; we don't have anything to give. When we do not have anything to provide our work, then success is unobtainable.

Put yourself first on the list. When you take care of yourself, then you can take care of others.

Make sure you do things that strengthen your body, mind, and soul first before you do anything else, for the benefit of everyone else.

Here are a few examples of self-care:

-Meditation

-Yoga

-Spending time with friends and family

-Spa day

-Going for walks alone or with others

-Developing a routine to help you with managing everything on your to-do list

-Exercise/healthy diet

-Sleep and rise early for optimal personal time

-Taking breaks-even 5 minutes breaks can work wonders

-Saying no to others when necessary

-Being organized. Clutter will only add more stress

-Reading a good book

Treating yourself to what makes your soul happy will result in optimal work productivity. Giving yourself that wiggle room to make sure you are mentally and physically taken care of is a great way to get your head in the game. It would take more time to try to take care of others poorly due to your lack of self-care than to make a small amount of time each day to be refreshed for your battles to come. Your success depends on where you are at emotionally, physically, and mentally. Putting that before everything else can help give you the confidence to conquer each day, a small step at a time.

Chapter 9
Let Go of Things That Hold You Down:

We cannot grow as individuals if we have a thousand other things holding us back from taking a step forward. Some of these things may be ones we might realize and others we don't even know that are holding us back. For instance, my fear held me back from pursuing what I wanted for many years. If I had known how to let go of fear back then, I might have started college sooner.

Our first step into freeing ourselves from oppressive baggage is to assess what we need to let go of and what is holding us back. Acknowledging your issue or pain and moving on is the only way to strive forward. Otherwise, you are only going to regress to a state of mind that will not benefit your happiness or success.

Our perception of perfection may include our family, house, children, attire, etc. We need to break that understanding of perfection by realizing that it does not exist. Everything has flaws. Understanding, accepting, developing weaknesses into strengths, and having confidence in such is the closest way we can come close to a perfect.

What might seem like a perfect life to you may be perceived differently in comparison to someone else. So, the real question boils down to, 'How can we break the cycle of perception?' How can we change how we view ourselves based on the opinions of others? The feeling of doing everything perfectly can consume your thoughts and mentally drain you for something that rests on someone else's point of view.

CLOSED MENTALITY

Becoming more open-minded to everything that comes into your life is the key to becoming a more understanding person. Having a closed-minded mentality will only limit you from seeing other people's perceptions. These perceptions can be beautiful lessons to integrate into your own life. They can help you grow as well as take into consideration the growth of others. Usually, closed-minded people are stubborn, and it is complicated to have disagreements with them. They don't like doing things differently or listen to new ideas. We are all naturally predisposed to having a closed mindset to keep ourselves emotionally protected. But our openness can define our inner truth, and without taking external considerations into our lives, we may never find the truth we all seek.

RESENTMENT/GRUDGES

The sooner you forgive, the better it is for you and your inner peace. It is only human to struggle with forgiveness. It's an uphill battle that can make or break a person. Recognizing the difference between being a victim or a survivor of your troubles is the first step to having control of this remission.

Also, ending your blame, whether it is on you or someone else is another step into getting to a better state of mind. This does not mean forgetting what something or someone did to you, but instead putting into perspective that blaming will only take from you, whether that's physical, emotional, mental, etc., and will never build you up. Blame is like a parasite; it will survive off of you by taking more of you away from yourself.

Taking every day to realize your resilience is the action we must take in defeating blame.

Next, we must forgive. A lot of times, we think because the other party is not sorry, we have an excuse to hold a grudge. On the contrary, forgiving the other person or situation to free yourself is the primary way to dignify your struggle and pain. Mahatma Gandhi once said, "The weak can never forgive. Forgiveness is the attribute of the strong." We can take that teaching and put it in the viewpoint of our lives to choose the person we want to be through absolution.

TOXIC RELATIONSHIPS

These include relationships in general: a friend, spouse, family member, co-worker, etc. You have to know when that relationship is not suitable for you and your health. Some people drain your life completely, and they don't realize it sometimes. As sympathetic as you may be to that person, it is not your responsibility to save them from their toxicity. It's your responsibility to take care of yourself just as much as the other person is liable for taking care of themselves.

It is up to you to acknowledge it and make a change. You don't have to get into an argument or be rude to them. You can distance yourself from that person. It can get more complicated than that when it comes to a spouse or a close family member, but you are responsible for your own life and happiness. You can't live miserable to make someone else happy.

WORRYING

Can you change whatever you are worrying about? Whether you can or cannot, then there is no point in being troubled because we have the power of controlling the situation or we have the power of letting the situation go. Worrying comes from fear and anxiety. I have been dealing with fear and anxiety for most of my life. The difference is now, I control it, and it doesn't control me how it used to. I wasted so much of my time and energy, worrying about things that didn't matter and didn't happen. We miss the most precious moments of our life because we let our worry cloud our vision. Having control over our feelings gives us the power to assert ourselves in our own lives and issues.

OTHER PEOPLE PERCEPTIONS/OPINIONS ABOUT YOU

What others think of you it is not your problem, it is theirs. Most of the time, their opinion of you is entirely wrong. They say things how they see it, not how they are in reality. Honestly, some people feel the need to have an opinion about everything and everyone. It's just how they are. It doesn't have anything to do with you. We ultimately have the choice to let these perceptions control everything we do. The moment we choose to let go of these exterior opinions is the moment we decide to live our lives for ourselves.

TRYING TO PLEASE EVERYONE

If you decide to please everyone, you will suffer as a result. You will say and do things that are going to be against what you believe and think. By trying to please other people, we disrespect ourselves, our struggles, and everything we have worked for. We need to start by finding the confidence in ourselves. Tell yourself every day the good things about yourself- the things on the inside that you find to be the most admirable. After you've gone through them all, remind yourself that these are the reasons you trust your own hearts and not the intention of others. It may seem silly or minuscule at first, but continuously enforcing that into your life will give you the motivation to go against the flow.

TAKING EVERYTHING PERSONALLY

If someone has been mean/rude to you, forgive them and don't take it personally. Maybe it didn't have anything to do with you. Perhaps they are having a terrible day, and they wanted to vent to someone. It is not fair, but it happens more than often. People sometimes have bad days. It is not ok, and it should not give everyone a free pass to be rude to others just because they are having a bad day. Although bad behavior isn't always justifiable, by putting yourself in the other person's shoes, you gain insight into why they acted the way they did. This allows you to further empathize with them, which is the first step to moving on.

ANGER

Feeling angry all the time is not suitable for your soul. It just takes away from your happiness and drains your energy. First, you need to acknowledge WHY you are mad or angry. Then, you need to validate your feelings from yourself. Sometimes getting angry is okay. It is a human emotion we all have, and if we didn't get mad sometimes, then no one would stand up for anything- no one would fight for anything. But in the cases where we see it get the best of us, we need to take a look at our situation and assess. We need to know its okay to have these feelings and remind ourselves that it does not control us.

Sometimes we might feel anger toward someone, and we don't know where it is coming from. Once you find out why you can work towards letting go because it just doesn't serve you.

12 Principles Of Personal Growth

CONTROL

As much as we want to have authority in every situation, we don't have a say in some parts of our life. If we come across the word control, we should not perceive it as being in command of the situation but rather as how we manage the parts of our lives that we have control over in a healthy way to make the uncontrollable easier to deal with. As much as you try, some things are out of your control.

THE PAST

Stop dwelling about what has already happened; it's in the past, leave it in the past. It's okay to think about it because it is a part of your story, but when we let it consume our lives, it can destroy us. I hear this a lot when people keep bringing up their history and the things they did or didn't do. I feel like it is such a waste of time and energy to be talking or dwelling on the past. You cannot turn back time, can you? Instead, invest your time and energy into something useful like the present time.

THE FUTURE

We are not there yet! Let go of your worry about what's going to happen in the future. It has not happened yet, and it might not happen at all. So don't worry about it. The anxious feeling of what's going to happen and the overthinking of every little thing will go away in time when we decide to focus our thoughts on the present. We waste precious energy and time when we worry and don't focus on the present. We also miss a lot of opportunities because we are overthinking and overanalyzing what's going to happen.

THE NEED TO ALWAYS BE RIGHT

You don't always have to make someone else see your point of view. Having your own opinions should be enough without explanations. Sometimes you can't force someone to agree with you about everything.

PAST FAILURES

Whether you have experienced a failed relationship, marriage, or business venture, learn from it. Look at it as proper teaching lessons instead. You can choose to see them as failures, or you can see the positive life lessons out of them. Everything happens for a reason. We make our mistakes as a way for us to learn from them.

So, to flourish in our own time and space, we need to let go of the past, exterior criticism and all negative forces. We need to remind ourselves daily that we can create magic and have confidence in doing so. The sooner we learn this, the sooner we can succeed.

Chapter 10
Embrace Challenge

> "*If it doesn't challenge you, it does not change you.*"
> - Fred DeVito.

Evaluate where you are and where you want to be. If you are not happy where you are in your life right now, it is time to change that. Often, changes come with a lot of challenges as well. For example, maybe you don't like your job. To improve that, you might need to get a higher degree or leave your job and apply somewhere else, which can be challenging because there are a few things that you need to take into consideration. These can be elements such as expenses, time, and other responsibilities. There may be challenges that make achieving your goal seem impossible but building the courage to do so will pay you back in abundance. You have to leave your comfort zone, and that is challenging to do. But if you embrace the challenge and make it part of the journey, it won't look so impossible.

That's why people often step back and are afraid to do what they want to.

If you never challenge yourself, you are going to be stuck in the same circle you are in right now. Whenever one stops challenging themselves, they also stop growing as an individual. We all love our comfort zone. Doesn't it feel nice? Why change something or do something else if where we are at is good enough?

You have a beautiful house, nice car, and you have a good-paying job. It is a beautiful thing; many people would love to have that. But you hate what you do every day.

You hate that you need to leave every morning, rush, and deal with traffic jams. Then after a long day of working at a place, you don't like, with people you're probably don't care about much, it is 6:00 pm. You come home, exhausted, and the only thing you want to do is lie down and relax. You can't do that because you have a spouse that wants your attention and missed you all day long. You may have kids that are super excited to finally see you home and spend a few moments with you. Then, it's time for bed and do this all over again. Same job, same people, same struggles, the same dissatisfactions, and same guilt feeling for not spending enough time with your family on repeat until the end.

Or you can challenge yourself to change. Change your career. Get a higher education. Open your own business. Anything can be achieved when you challenge yourself with an opportunity to do so.

To embrace challenge means that you are not scared to move forward no matter what difficulties you run into.

We need to practice looking at change as an opportunity rather than a place you're uncomfortable in. Without making a change in your life, then progressing in anything is impossible. If you don't decide to advance, then nothing will change. Our biggest challenge in life is change, but we forget that change means growth. Having faith in yourself to flourish in the circumstances you are in and obtaining the confidence to evolve; then you have already won your battle. You have already succeeded.

Chapter 11
Do a SWOT Analysis on Yourself

Usually, a S.W.O.T (strength, weaknesses, opportunities, threats) analysis is done on companies to evaluate their business plans and help them come up with strategies for the planning process. It helps an organization identify its strengths and weaknesses while determining its threats and opportunities.

But this analysis can be done on a personal level as well and can be helpful to get to know your self a little bit more in-depth.

You can start by answering the following questions about yourself. Then, based on the answers, you can see the areas you need to work on more (weaknesses and threats) and areas that are to your advantage (opportunities and strengths).

Strengths:

What are your strengths?

Every person is good at something. What are you good at?

What is your expertise?

What do you enjoy doing?

Are you trustworthy?

Are you dependable?

Are you a good listener?

What are your advantages?

What is your education level?

What are your other skills?

What resources do you have?

What life experiences do you have that are valuable?

Weaknesses:

Do you have any wrong/negative habits?

Do you have self-doubt?

Do you have a lack of confidence?

What are your fears/doubts?

What areas are you lacking?

Do you need more training or education in specific areas?

Opportunities:

Here are a few questions you can ask yourself to find out opportunities:

What can you change?

What can you improve?

What steps should you take to make it happen?

How can you turn any of your strengths into opportunities?

Threats:

What obstacles do you face?

What is changing in your life real-life professional experience?

Do you feel like you are competing with others?

What obligation do you have in life right now that would prevent you and your personal development?

Answer the questions that apply to you and look at your answers.

Based on the SWOT analysis, you can modify different strategies to make choices and changes for your life and your growth.

Chapter 12
Stop Judging Yourself and Start Observing

If you always judge yourself for everything you do or the way you perform your tasks, you are always putting yourself down, which leads to doubting yourself for everything you want to do.

Instead, observe the way you speak, do things, and treat others. Then you can improve anything you feel like you need to improve on.

If you have a fixed mindset:

-You will take every feedback personally.

-There is no room or possibility for change (in your mind).

-You will always choose your comfort zone over being challenged.

-You quit every time things get complicated.

-You feel jealous of other people's achievements.

Examples of a growth mindset are:

-You can change and grow.

-You look at past failures as teaching moments.

-You try again- when you first don't succeed.

-You listen to feedback and constructive criticism.

-You don't have any limits on what you can achieve.

-You get inspired by the success that other people around you have achieved.

-You love to be challenged.

This simple analysis can be easily integrated into your daily mindset. It's an excellent way of assessing relationships, decisions, and everyday issues. Putting this into practice can assist our self-awareness to round ourselves out as a person. The more balanced we are, the easier we can achieve our goals.

Creating a healthy mindset that includes organization, and attainable goals will not only help you chase your dreams but also find success in the smallest of accomplishments. Building the courage to think outside of your personal realm and ignoring external elements will take time, but in doing so, you can help free yourself of the factors that hold you down. We all struggle with getting started on achieving our ambitions, but we all share this common desire to want to release ourselves from self-doubt. Knowing that you're not the only one feeling this way can be a big help in building your confidence.

Remember your drive. Focus on what you want to change for the better. Tread your path with the grace and confidence you deserve to have and succeed with determination from within yourself.

Bonus

My favorite quotes about personal growth:

"It is never too late for a new beginning in your life."
- Joyce Meyers

"Continued improvement is better than delayed perfection."
- Mark Twain

"It seems impossible until it's done."
- Nelson Mandela

"Change is painful, but nothing is as painful as being stuck somewhere you don't belong."
- N.R Narayana Murthy

"The 3 C's of life: change, chances, choices."
- Zig Ziglar

"Difficult roads often lead to beautiful destinations."
- Zig Ziglar

"Work hard in silence ... let your success be the noise."
- Frank Ocean

"The best way to predict your future is to create it."
- Abraham Lincoln

"I am building from every mistake I have made."
- Mandy Hale

12 Principles Of Personal Growth

"Fear is a reaction ... courage is a decision."
- Sir Winston Churchill

"Do what you have to do until you can do what you want to do."
- Oprah Winfrey

"The best investment is an investment in yourself."
- Warren Buffet

Acknowledgments

Many thanks to everyone that contributed to bringing this book to life.

-Sabrina Liburdi

-Book Designer -Armejndi

-Self-Publishing School Community

About The Author

Anisa Marku is the author of The Art Of Setting S.M.A.R.T Goals and the founder of My Third Culture Kid.

She is Albanian who grew up in Germany and moved to Michigan 15 years ago. As a high school dropout, her future didn't feel very secure until she decided to set achievable goals for herself and turn her life and career around. Anisa started college ten years later and graduated in June 2017.

With a passion for motivating and inspiring others, she is now working on building her online enterprise and pursuing her passion as a writer.

NOW IT'S YOUR TURN

Discover the EXACT 3-step blueprint you need to become a bestselling author in 3 months. Self-Publishing School helped me, and now I want them to help you with this FREE WEBINAR!

Even if you're busy, bad at writing, or don't know where to start, you CAN write a bestseller and build your best life.

With tools and experience across a variety of niches and professions, Self-Publishing School is the only resource you need to take your book to the finish line!

DON'T WAIT

Watch this FREE WEBINAR now, and
Say "YES" to becoming a bestseller:

https://xe172.isrefer.com/go/affegwebinar/bookbrosinc7367/
Click on "Join Our Free Training"

Can You Help?

Thank You For Reading My Book!

I appreciate all of your feedback, and I love hearing what you have to say.

I need your input to make the next version of this book and my future books better.

Please leave me an honest review on Amazon letting me know what you thought of the book.

Thanks so much!
Anisa Marku

www.ingramcontent.com/pod-product-compliance
Lightning Source LLC
Chambersburg PA
CBHW051411290426
44108CB00015B/2239